Written by John Parsons

Contents   Page

Rigby

Chapter Snapshots

"Airports are busy places,

filled with busy people."

Introduction

Airports are busy places, filled with busy people. What might you see inside an airport? In one part, families may be waving good-bye to each other. In another, friends may be greeting passengers. Some business people may be traveling to work in another city. Other people may be arriving for a vacation or about to go home after a vacation.

Domestic And International Flights

Domestic flights take place in and around the U.S. The planes usually leave from domestic gates or terminals. International flights take passengers to other countries. These planes usually leave from international gates or terminals.

At the airport, there are hundreds of people working quickly. Their jobs are to make sure that passengers, their luggage, and the aircraft arrive and depart on time.

In this book, we meet some of the people who help passengers arrive and depart safely.

1. Check-In

At this airport, the first passengers for the day arrive at 5.00 a.m. Every passenger starts their journey by checking in.

At the ticket counter, the ticket agent greets each passenger. The agent checks the first passenger's ticket to make sure the information is correct.

The ticket counter

A passenger checks in.

A ticket agent checks the ticket.

The agent asks some questions and for a photo identification.

The agent prints out tags to put on the passenger's bags. The tags list the flight information. The bags should now arrive at the same airport as the passenger!

Airport Codes

Every baggage tag has a special three-letter code on it. Every airport in the world has its own code so bags are sent to the right airport.

Bags going to the Los Angeles airport have a tag with the code "LAX." Bags going to Chicago have a tag with the code "ORD." Here are some airport codes:

Los Angeles:	LAX
Chicago:	ORD
Miami:	MIA
Boston:	BOS

Usually, passengers like to keep a small bag with them. The agent checks to make sure the bag won't take up too much space inside the aircraft.

Sometimes, people want to take very large items with them. The agent tells the passengers why they are not allowed to take up too much space inside the aircraft. Can you imagine a surfboard or a bicycle sitting beside you?

An airline agent

The agent asks each passenger if they want a seat next to a window or the aisle. Using a computer, the agent then gives the passenger a seat number.

Lots Of Seats!

Getting everybody into the right seats in an aircraft can be a big job. On large aircraft, such as a Boeing 747–400, there can be up to 421 passengers!

The Right Seat

The airline knows that business travelers like to have aisle seats, and that families and people on vacation like to have window seats. They also like to make sure that people traveling together have seats next to each other.

On every aircraft, there are special seats for people with disabilities or special medical needs. On these seats, the arm rests can be removed to help the passengers get in and out of his or her seat.

As soon as the passenger has been given a seat number, the computer prints out a boarding pass. The boarding pass is handed to the passenger. The agent also reviews the departure information.

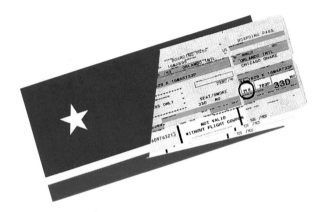

A Boarding Pass

The passenger's bags are placed onto a moving belt behind the check-in counter. Then the bags move through a small door.

Once the passenger reaches the departure gate, it's time to relax. But other airport workers are *not* relaxing!

2. Baggage-Handling

At this airport, there are about 80 flights each day to airports around the country and the world. That means thousands of bags are handled every day.

The airlines take extra care that passengers' bags arrive at the right airport at the right time. After the bags move away from the check-in counter, they roll down into the baggage-handling area.

It is noisy, and
very busy inside the
baggage-handling area.

Every bag tag is checked
by a baggage handler.
Then the baggage handlers
place the bags on the right
trailer.

Small trucks pull the long chains of trailers from the baggage-handling area to the right aircraft. For safety, the workers wear brightly colored clothing so the truck drivers can see them.

Fragile Baggage

Sometimes passengers' baggage contain items that are fragile or easily broken. Colorful stickers with FRAGILE on them are stuck on the baggage.

FRAGILE

For large aircraft, bags may be put into huge metal containers that fit into the hold.

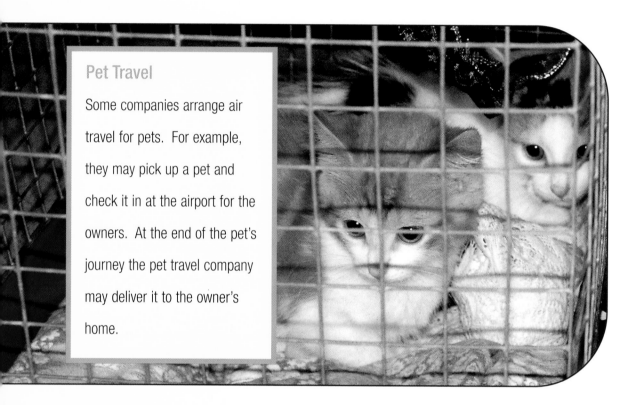

Pet Travel

Some companies arrange air travel for pets. For example, they may pick up a pet and check it in at the airport for the owners. At the end of the pet's journey the pet travel company may deliver it to the owner's home.

Animals in cages are carefully placed on the trailers. The baggage handlers always tell the pilots if there are live animals in their aircraft's hold. When there are animals on board, the pilots turn on the heaters to keep them warm during the flight.

It is also the job of the baggage handlers to unload bags arriving from other airports.

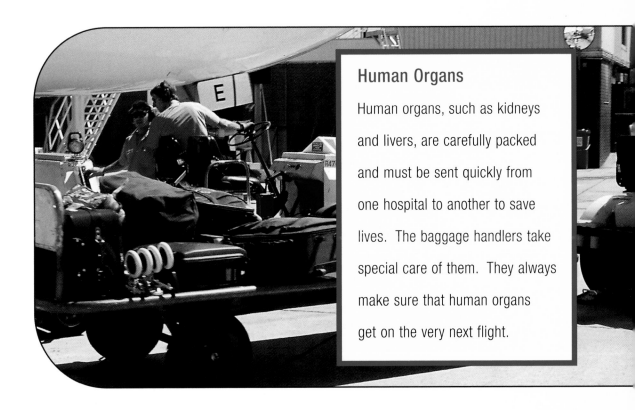

Human Organs

Human organs, such as kidneys and livers, are carefully packed and must be sent quickly from one hospital to another to save lives. The baggage handlers take special care of them. They always make sure that human organs get on the very next flight.

Trailers full of bags arrive at the baggage-handling area. They are quickly unloaded onto another conveyor belt. This conveyor belt moves the bags into the arrivals area. Here, the passengers who have just arrived can pick up their bags.

3. Preparing Meals

Close to this airport, people prepare meals in a huge kitchen. These people start preparing delicious meals and snacks for passengers from 4:00 a.m.

Meals are prepared in clean, hygienic areas, and everyone wears clean coats and hair nets.

In this kitchen, over 10,000 meals are prepared every day! During holidays, even more people travel, so more meals are needed.

Many Meals

To make sure that passengers traveling on more than one flight don't eat the same meals, they are changed often. The kitchen team makes six different types of each meal: breakfast, lunch, and dinner. They also make six different types of snacks for morning, afternoon, and after dinner.

As flights leave at different times, fresh meals and snacks are prepared throughout the day. The video screens show all the flights that are leaving each day.

New Meals

Sometimes the airline managers ask for a new kind of meal. Sikoi Tawa, the Head Chef, will prepare many new meals for the airline managers to taste. When they choose one, they'll say, "That's just perfect!"

Sikoi Tawa is preparing meals to put into the meal carts.

After the food is cooked, it is quickly cooled down. To help the kitchen staff know how to present the meals, there are photographs of each meal on the walls. The food is placed onto trays, covered, and stored in large carts.

The carts are loaded onto trucks and driven to the airport. Once on the aircraft, the meals are heated again. They are still in perfect condition.

Special Meals

Special meals must be ordered when you buy your ticket.
Sometimes passengers ask for special meals to be made for their children.
Other special meals are prepared for many reasons.

Vegetarian:	Meals with no meat or dairy products.
Lacto-Vegetarian:	Meals with no meat, but with dairy products.
Diabetic:	Meals with very low amounts of sugar.
Low Fat:	Meals with low amounts of fat and oil.
Low Cholesterol:	Meals with low amounts of cholesterol.
Muslim:	Meals with foods that Muslim people are allowed to eat.
Hindu:	Meals with foods that Hindu people are allowed to eat.
Kosher:	Meals with foods that are prepared in a Kosher kitchen.

VIP Meals

When a President or a VIP (Very Important Person) flies in an air force aircraft, the kitchen staff makes very special meals.

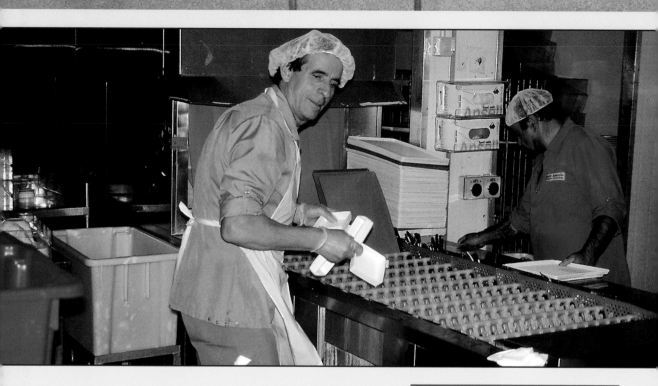

In another part of the kitchen is the scullery. The scullery is where the dirty dishes and cutlery are brought in from all the arriving planes.

Everything is sorted and then washed in huge dishwashers. In this scullery, about half a million dishes and pieces of cutlery are washed each week!

The Flight Crew's Meals

The airline's kitchen staff prepares meals for the pilots and the flight attendants.

Every aircraft has two pilots, but they eat different food — even different bread! If one pilot gets sick, the other pilot can safely fly the aircraft!

4. Turnaround

Baggage Trailer

Fuel Truck

Waste Truck

As soon as an aircraft lands, the airline workers know what to do. In 30-35 minutes they must get the aircraft ready quickly and safely for its next flight. This time is called "turnaround."

Meanwhile, the departing passengers are waiting inside the airport terminal.

Outside, on the tarmac, baggage trailers are driven up to the aircraft. The fuel truck and waste truck are also driven up alongside the aircraft. A truck from the kitchen is ready with the meals.

The truck drivers and the ground staff are very careful around the aircraft. They know that they must not stand behind or in front of the powerful engines. The engine's hot air can easily blow a person over.

When the passengers have left the aircraft, it is ready for turnaround.

An engineer begins by checking parts of the outside of the aircraft to make sure it is safe.

The fuel truck's hose is hooked up to the aircraft. It pumps fuel into the fuel tanks.

The waste truck's hose is hooked up to the aircraft. It empties out the toilets.

At one side of this aircraft, bags are unloaded and placed on empty trailers. Full trailers wait with new bags for loading on board.

On the other side of the aircraft, workers unload the used meal carts. Then carts with fresh meals and snacks are loaded from the kitchen's truck.

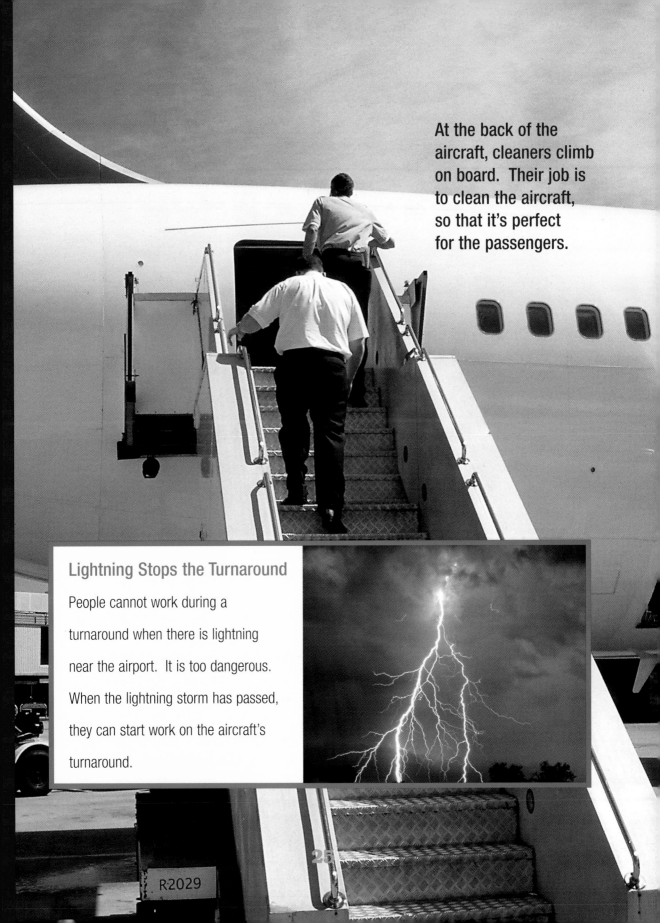

At the back of the aircraft, cleaners climb on board. Their job is to clean the aircraft, so that it's perfect for the passengers.

Lightning Stops the Turnaround

People cannot work during a turnaround when there is lightning near the airport. It is too dangerous. When the lightning storm has passed, they can start work on the aircraft's turnaround.

R2029

5. Flight Staff

Before the flight, the flight attendants meet with the Chief Flight Attendant. They talk about the passengers who need extra help. The flight attendants are told where they will stand for their safety demonstrations.

Then they are each asked an emergency safety question. Each flight attendant must remember what to do in every kind of emergency!

Safety Training: Flight Attendants

Flight attendants keep passengers safe and comfortable during a flight. As part of their training, they learn about first aid, what to do in an emergency, and about each aircraft's safety equipment.

Inside the aircraft, the flight attendants check the meal carts. They also check that there are plenty of magazines and newspapers for the passengers.

The Chief Flight Attendant talks about the flight with the pilots. The pilots know the route that they will fly the aircraft. They also know how long the flight will take. Before the flight, everyone does a final safety check.

Safety Training: Pilots

Pilots are trained for hundreds of hours before they can fly passenger aircraft. Every six months, each pilot does more training in a "simulator." It is like a huge, moving video game. The simulator looks and feels just like a real jet aircraft. Pilots learn what to do in every kind of emergency.

6. Ready For Take-Off!

The turnaround is finished. The flight attendants and the pilots are on board. The aircraft is safe and ready for boarding. Passengers are told that the aircraft is ready for boarding. At the departure gate, every boarding pass is checked by a flight attendant and the computer.

On board the aircraft, the passengers are greeted by the flight attendants and shown to their seats. Their small bags are put in safe places.

Did you know?

In the cockpit, the pilots have finished their safety check. They know the aircraft is safe to fly.

There are about 365 lights, switches, and gauges in a cockpit.

Outside the aircraft, the hold doors are shut tight, checked, and double-checked. Finally, when everyone is on board, the passenger doors are shut and checked as well.

The flight attendants check the comfort of the passengers. A safety video starts on the video screens. The flight attendants also demonstrate safety features of the aircraft.

The control tower has cleared the aircraft for take-off. A small truck pushes the aircraft backward, away from the departure gate. The pilot then drives the aircraft to the runway for take-off. The passengers relax. The jet engines roar.

Fun for Kids!

On most long flights, young children receive a free activity pack which contains things like books, pens, and games. They can also wear headphones to tune into a music program. On long flights, they can watch movies. Airlines always look after kids!

Official Airline of the 2000 Olympic Games

Back at the check-in counters, down in the baggage-handling area, outside the airport terminal, and over at the kitchen, hundreds of people are still working. They are getting ready for the next flight in and the next flight out. It's still only 7:00 a.m., and there's another 75 flights to work on before their day finishes, very late at night!

Index

Bookweb Links

Read more Bookweb 3 books about aircraft,
travel and adventure:

Action Safety — Nonfiction
Detector Dog — Nonfiction
Hugo And Splot — Fiction
Same Idea, Different Year — Fiction

Key To Bookweb
Fact Boxes

☐ **Arts**
☐ **Health**
☐ **Science**
☐ Social Studies
☐ **Technology**